This book gift to

....

....

....

WELCOMING RAMADAN FOR KIDS

Zabed Mohammad, PhD.
Educator & Researcher
Canada

info@kidseducare.ca
zabedm@kidseducare.ca

Library of Congress Cataloging-in-Publication Data
ISBN: 978-1-998923-08-3

Publisher
Kids Edu Care Inc.
Children's Dedicated Learning Series
Website: www.kidseducare.ca
Illustration Copyright © 2022 by
Kids Edu Care Inc.
Canada

Illustration & Design
Bee Digital

Ramadan is coming...
It is a special month for the whole
of humankind. Are we ready to
welcome Ramadan?

What do you mean? Why do we have to be ready to welcome Ramadan?

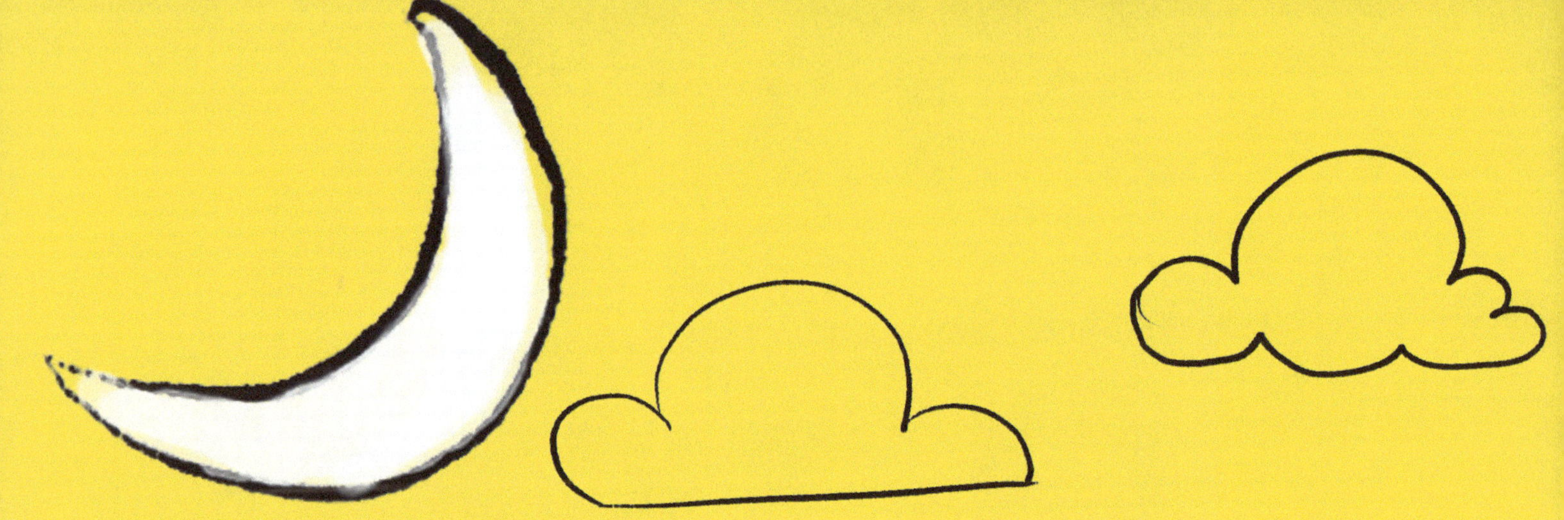

I am excited. Every evening, we have to start seeking the crescent moon in the western part of the sky.

Oh! Really? Why?
What does that mean?

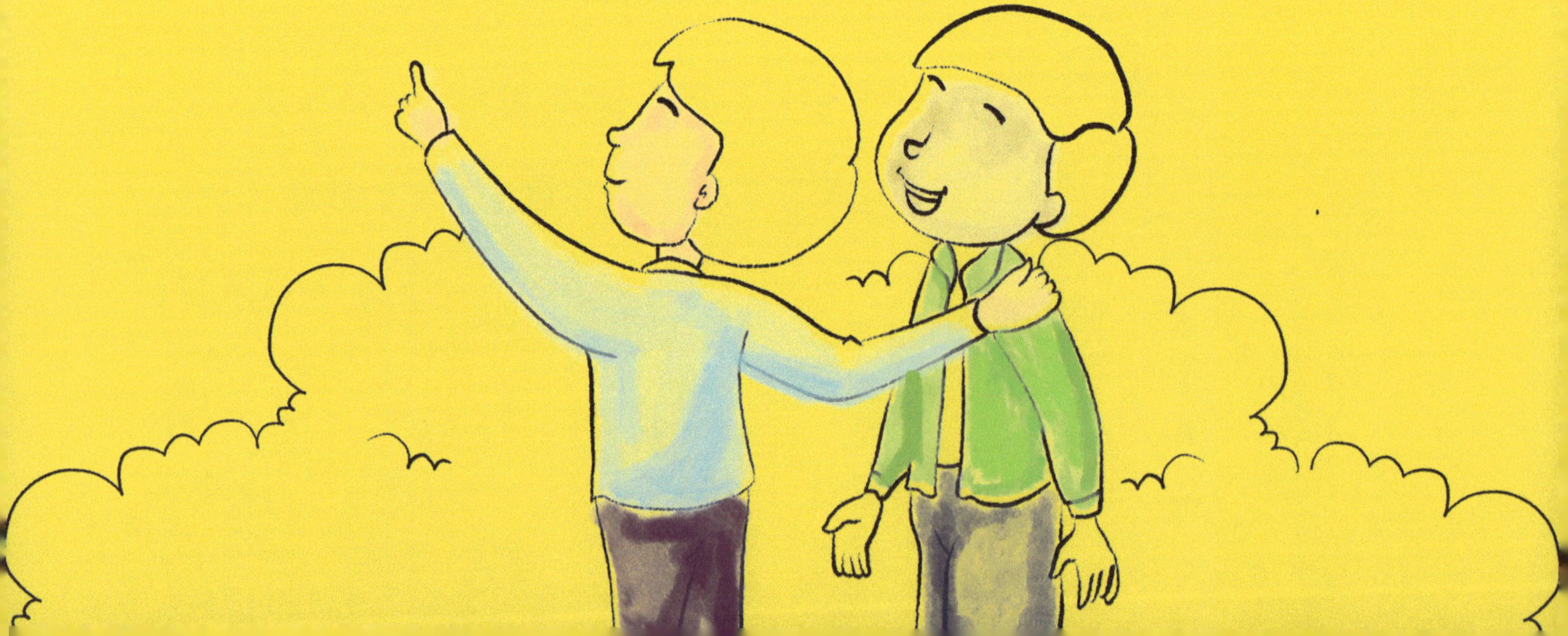

It means if we see the crescent Moon in the sky, we have to start fasting. Do you know what fasting is?
Not exactly!

Well. Do you know about Ramadan? It is a month of fasting, which means we cannot eat or drink between dawn and sunset.

Oh, I know! During Ramadan, my parents don't eat in the daytime.

Right! But what about you? Do you eat during the day of the month of Ramadan?

Yes, I do. I'm just seven, and so I can eat. During Ramadan, my mom cooks and prepares different delicious foods, and I love to eat them when I'm allowed.

Ah, I see. Ramadan means thirty days of fasting, but I am turning nine this year, and fasted for 15 days last year. I did not eat anything during the day at that time. I waited for sundown to break my fast and have Iftar with my mom, dad, and siblings.

But you could drink water or fruit juice, I think?

Oh, no! During Ramadan, we are not allowed to eat or drink anything for a certain time period.

Really? What do you mean, "a certain time period"?

Here I mean, before fazar Salah to Magrib Salah, or before the sun rises in the east until it sets in the west, we are not allowed to eat or drink anything.

Are you sure? It's been a long time. I get hungry very frequently, so my mom and dad allow me to eat and drink.

Yes, you are just seven, and that is why your mom and dad allow you to eat and drink. But my parents don't let me because I must practice fasting and other religious rituals.

It seems that your parents are stricter than mine! I am surprised, and I feel so bad for you.

Yes, I can realize that idea. But the facts
are different.

What do you mean? Why should we not eat for the whole day, and do it for a whole month?

Listen! My parents love me the way your parents love you. But Allah (SWT) loves us all too. We are all created by Allah (SWT), and we all have to go back to Allah (SWT), so we all have to follow Allah's (SWT) advice, which is given in the Holy Quran. Allah (SWT) declares: "O, you who believe! fasting is prescribed for you as it was for those before you, so that you will become mindful of Allah (SWT)." (Surah Al-Baqarah 2:183)

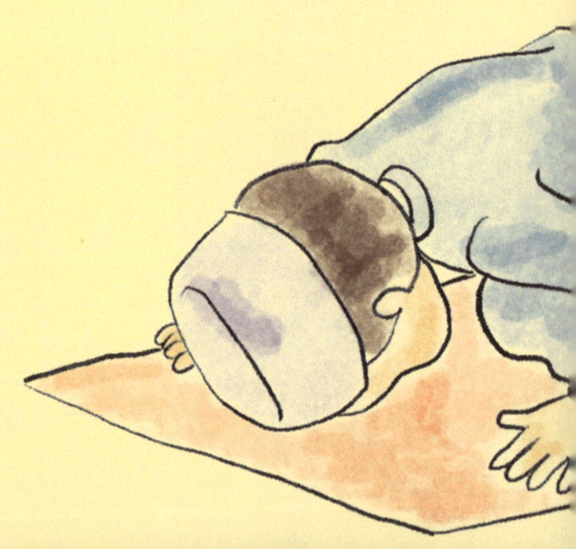

Well, the other day, my mom and dad said that in the month of Ramadan, the Holy Quran was revealed as guidance for everyone, and until the day of judgement, the Quran was considered as a constitution for the whole world.

Yes, they are right. As I mentioned earlier, Allah (SWT) advised us. We have no choice, and no matter whether our parents love us or not, we have to fast, except for children, the sick, or those with special health conditions. But it is sometimes challenging; since we feel hungry, sometimes we cannot concentrate on our studies, so we need preparation and practice. That is why at the beginning of Ramadan, the Prophet Muhammad (SAW) used to convey welcoming messages to the whole Ummah, just to prepare everybody.

Wow! Tell me how to prepare for Ramadan! What kind of preparations do we have to make?

Well, by reading books, listening to my parents, and having friday discussions with our Imam, I have learned a few things I can share! During Ramadan, for example, we need to reduce our workload.

That's very nice for everyone.
What else?

Not only that,
our Prophet Muhammad (SAW)
advises us to help the poor
as much as we can.

Yeah, my parents always help
our poorer relatives and other
people. These are good deeds.

I learned that we have to read the
Holy Quran to know each other better.
for example, who created us?
Who is the owner of this country?

Well, I know we came from
Allah (SWT). But we own our
own country, don't we?

It's an excellent question. You know what? Allah (SWT) is the owner of the whole Universe, including all countries and everything we see around us.

Really? How do you know that?

The Holy Quran
explains all of
these things,
what is ours
and what is not.
Hey, let's read the Holy Quran together!
I am sure you will find all this information.

What do you mean by all this
information?

I mean, since the Holy Quran comes from Allah (SWT), it contains all the information we need in this world. So, I would say reading the Quran helps us to learn about ourselves.

Wow!

In addition, during the odd-numbered nights of the last ten days of Ramadan, there is one especially powerful night: Laylatul Qadar night.
Do you know what Laylatul Qadar night is?

I remember this. My parents prayed the whole night. But I don't know much about it!

Laylatul Qadar is a very important night, as that night Allah (SWT) declares and fulfills the Holy Quran as a guideline for all humans and the end of the Holy Quran, which was sent to our Prophet Muhammad (SAW) over a period of **23** years.The Holy Quran is the only book containing information about which there can be no doubt. Therefore, nothing can be added or edited, and there is never any need for changes.

Yes, my parents always read the Holy Quran. I also read it. My parents expect that someday I will memorize it, so I try hard to study it every day.

Wow, that's good. The Holy Quran is the word of Allah (SWT). As the creator, Allah (SWT) knows what we need or do not need, and that is why He (SWT) gave it to us.

Huh! So that's why my mom and dad always encourage me to read the Holy Quran, and why they read it every day!

Due to the Holy Quran, the month of
Ramadan is honoured. Another fact is,
Ramadan is a time for practicing
patience and increasing our Iman.

Clearly your mom and dad
carry on the same traditions
that my mom and dad do.

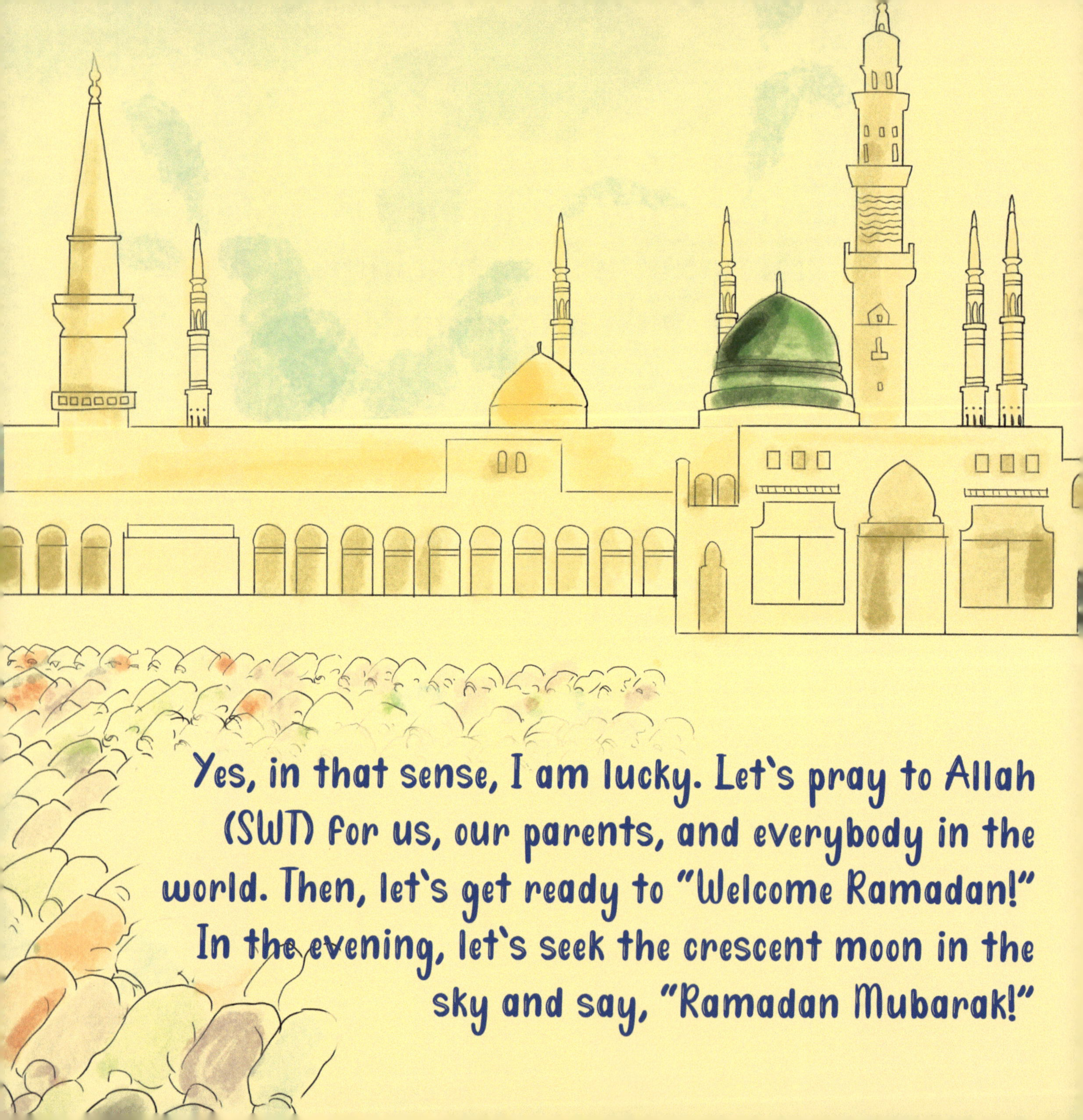

Yes, in that sense, I am lucky. Let's pray to Allah (SWT) for us, our parents, and everybody in the world. Then, let's get ready to "Welcome Ramadan!" In the evening, let's seek the crescent moon in the sky and say, "Ramadan Mubarak!"

Other great books by Zabed Mohammad!
We hope you like them!

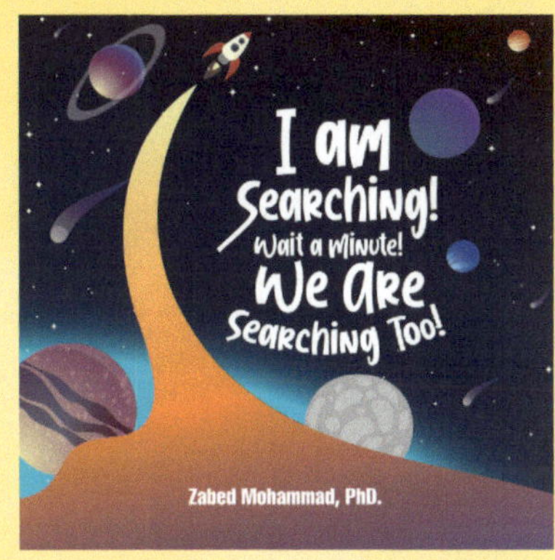

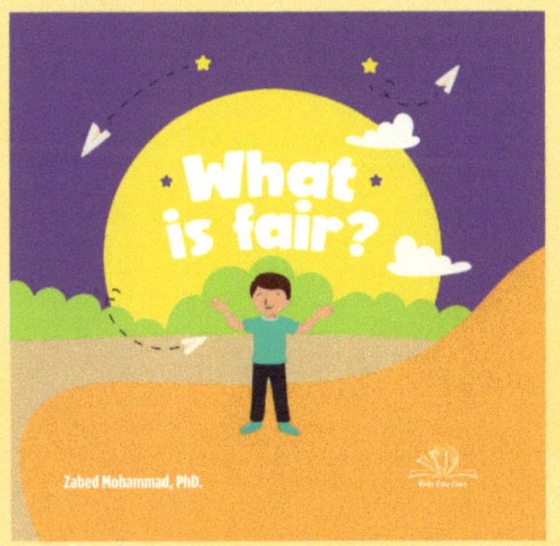

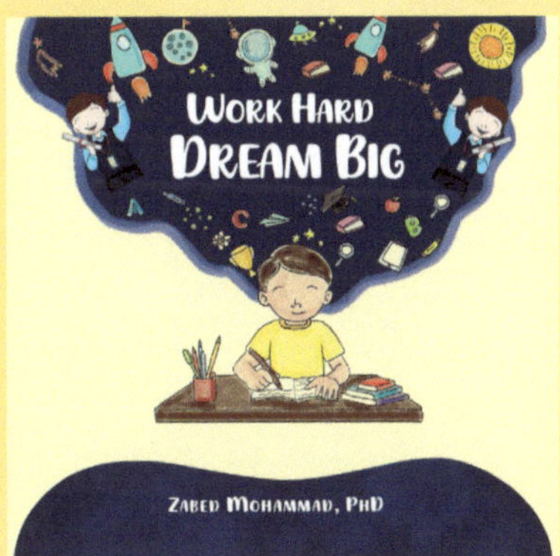

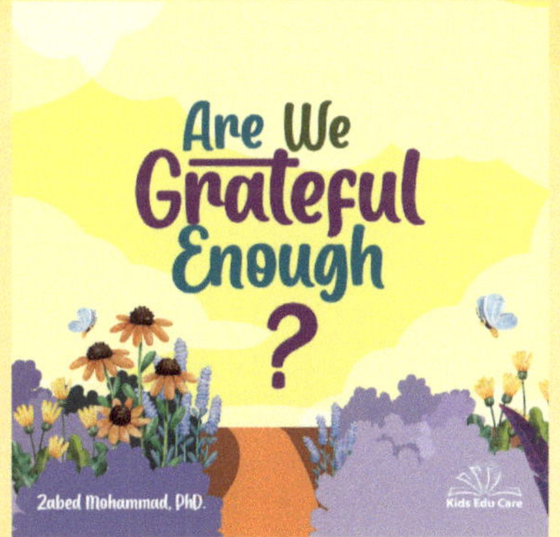